"I SINCERELY HOPE
THAT THE MUSEUM WILL BE
A CONTINUING SOURCE OF
INSPIRATION AND EDUCATION
FOR ALL TIME, AND THAT
THE GARDENS AND GROUNDS
WILL THEMSELVES BE A COUNTRY
PLACE MUSEUM WHERE VISITORS
MAY ENJOY AS I HAVE, NOT
ONLY THE FLOWERS, TREES, AND
SHRUBS, BUT ALSO THE SUNLIT
MEADOWS, SHADY WOOD PATHS,
AND THE PEACE AND QUIET
CALM OF A COUNTRY PLACE
WHICH HAS BEEN LOVED AND
TAKEN CARE OF FOR
THREE GENERATIONS."

Henry Francis du Pont

Discover the
Winterthur Estate

by Pauline K. Eversmann
with Kathryn H. Head

Table of Contents

The Early Winterthur Estate. 1

Creating a Country Place 9

From Country Place to Grand Estate. 19

A Country Place Museum. 33

Addendum
Winterthur Genealogy 43

The Early Winterthur Estate

*F*rom the moment visitors enter Winterthur's grounds, they encounter tangible reminders of Winterthur's past. Rolling meadows, man-made ponds, stone bridges, greenhouses, dairy barns, golf course greens, and workers' housing all testify to the days in the late nineteenth and early twentieth centuries when Winterthur was not yet a museum but a thriving country estate. As we near the end of the twentieth century, when such large estates are increasingly rare, routinely broken up into smaller, more manageable parcels of land, it may require a great deal of imagination to conjure up a time when Winterthur encompassed more than 2,000 acres—acres that supported a herd of dairy cattle; beef cattle, sheep, and hogs for meat; extensive orchards; a poultry operation; a five-acre vegetable garden; fields of hay, wheat, barley, corn, and alfalfa to help feed the livestock; and more than 250 people. It also boasted its own train station; saw mill; milk bottling plant; carpenter, paint, and machine shops; and post office.

Yet this was the general configuration of the Winterthur estate in 1914, when Henry Algernon du Pont named his son the manager of the Winterthur Farms. Henry Francis du Pont, then a thirty-four-year-old bachelor, assumed control of the day-to-day operations of the farm, which represented a natural extension of his lifelong love for and devotion to the place of his birth. He eagerly embraced the opportunity to continue his

Henry Francis du Pont
Born at Winterthur, Henry Francis du Pont (1880–1969) was named manager of the Winterthur Farms in 1914. Cultivation of the Winterthur estate (which included not only supervising the extensive farming operations but also managing the gardens and directing the many house expansions required to accommodate his growing collection of antiques) became du Pont's lifelong career.

Left: Front pond at Winterthur.

I

**Pierre Samuel
du Pont de Nemours**

The son of a Parisian watchmaker, Pierre Samuel du Pont
de Nemours was a French
publisher and economist. The
patriarch of the du Pont family
in America, he instilled in his
sons a love of the land that
would profoundly influence
their activities in America.

Eleuthère Irénée du Pont

The younger son of Pierre
Samuel, Eleuthère Irénée
du Pont arrived in America on
New Year's Day 1800 and within two years established a black
powder manufactory along the
Brandywine River.

family's careful stewardship of the land. He
applied to this task the skills he had already
demonstrated while collaborating with his
father on the development of the naturalisti-
cally landscaped garden and would later
demonstrate on his own in amassing a world-
famous collection of American decorative
arts: strict attention to detail, continual
experimentation to achieve the desired goal,
and, above all, an unwillingness to accept
anything less than perfection.

In this dedication to the development
and preservation of the land, du Pont carried
on a devotion to agriculture that had become
a hallmark of the du Pont family since the
late eighteenth century in France. The
Winterthur estate that du Pont began to
manage in 1914 had been in his family's possession since the early nineteenth century.
Pierre Samuel du Pont de Nemours, born the
son of a Parisian watchmaker in 1739,
became a printer and developed an interest in
agriculture, aligning himself with a group of
French philosophers called the "Physiocrats,"
who believed in the importance of an agricultural economy and advocated finding true
happiness through tilling the soil. In 1774 he
purchased a small farm called Bois-des-Fossés
and raised his family amid 400 acres of fields,
gardens, orchards, and livestock herds. His
younger son, Eleuthère Irénée, joined the
family's printing firm in Paris but found the
urban environment as well as the political
turmoil of the French Revolution not only
dangerous but oppressive and longed to
return to the peaceful existence of the family

farm. In 1797 he wrote to his wife, who was living at Bois-des-Fossés with their children, "Oh, how happy we would be, my Sophie, away from the volcano on which we live and established in the *promised land.*"

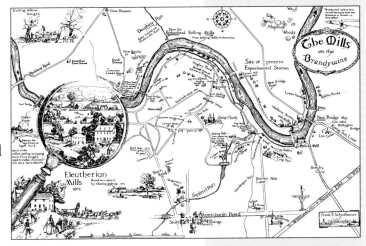

3

For Eleuthère Irénée and his father, the "promised land" was the new United States, in particular the state of Virginia, where they dreamed of establishing an agricultural colony near the proposed city of Washington. To fulfill this dream, the son studied botany and the father enlisted the support of investors to fund their proposed land development project. On January 1, 1800, following a difficult sea voyage, Pierre Samuel and his two sons and their families landed in America, settling initially in New Jersey. When the proposed Virginia project did not prove feasible, they set their sights further north and decided to settle on the banks of the Brandywine River in northern Delaware. There, drawing on skills Eleuthère Irénée learned during an apprenticeship with French chemist Lavoisier, they established a black powder manufactory. The Brandywine was a perfect site for a manufacturing enterprise: originating in the Welsh hills of eastern

Life on the Brandywine

Fertile land and proximity to ports in Philadelphia and Baltimore made the Brandywine Valley an attractive destination for early settlers. French immigrant Eleuthère Irénée du Pont selected a site near the Pennsylvania-Delaware line where he could harness the enormous potential of the Brandywine River to power his black powder factory, which he named Eleutherian Mills.

4

Henry Algernon du Pont

Following a distinguished career in the United States Army, Henry Algernon du Pont assumed management of the Winterthur property in 1876. The "Colonel," as he was often called, transformed the prospering gentleman's farm created by the Bidermanns into a grand American country estate.

Pennsylvania, the swiftly flowing river drops more than 120 feet before emptying into Delaware Bay in Wilmington, Delaware.

Once the powder plant, named E. I. du Pont de Nemours and Co., was in operation, the du Ponts turned their attention to their first love: land and agriculture. After building a family home on a hill above the mill and developing extensive gardens around it, Eleuthère Irénée began to acquire land, starting with the purchase of the nearby Martin farm with the intent of developing a herd of Merino sheep. In subsequent years, he added the Clenny Farm to the family's land holdings. These two acquisitions became the nucleus of the Winterthur estate, which was purchased from the family by Eleuthère Irénée's son-in-law, Jacques Antoine Bidermann, in 1837. Bidermann and his wife, Evelina Gabrielle du Pont, built a three-story Greek revival house on this land and moved there in 1839, immediately beginning the active development of the land into a working farm. They named the estate Winterthur after a town in Switzerland, the ancestral home of the Bidermanns. The rich soil of the Brandywine Valley, combined with effective agricultural management, enabled Evelina to write to a friend five years after moving to Winterthur, "Everything here grows wonderfully. You would be surprised to see the young orchard and the corn in it . . . We will have peaches in our garden this year and an abundance of strawberries . . . We also have green peas . . . Yesterday we had ninety-two hills of sweet potatoes planted. We bid fair also to have a fine crop of turkeys. The ducks are also coming on well, the chickens not so well."

The Bidermanns' son and only heir, James Irénée, who was living in France, agreed to sell the property to Evelina's brother, Henry du Pont, upon the deaths of his parents in 1863 and 1865. He wrote to his uncle, "I am satisfied to think that the Winterthur estate shall remain in the family. I am sure now that all my father's works will be respected and continued if possible." Henry du Pont purchased Winterthur not for his own use but for that of his children. His older son, Henry Algernon du Pont, took up residence at Winterthur in 1875 after resigning his post as a colonel in the United States Army. He had married Pauline Foster a year earlier and now turned his full attention to the development of the Winterthur estate.

Henry Algernon did, indeed, continue the work begun by his aunt and uncle. He added more land to the estate, began a dairy herd, extended the garden surrounding the house, developed an arboretum of conifers, and enlarged the house twice, first adding a fourth story and a new roofline and then, in 1902, building a large wing across the front of the existing structure. In addition, he had many of the farm buildings redesigned so that they presented a somewhat uniform look: front porches with Tuscan columns, stepped brick cornices under the rooflines, dormer windows with columns, and stuccoed exteriors painted olive green. A train station, gatehouse, and many miles of new roads were other improvements made to the property by Henry Algernon.

5

Evolution of the Winterthur House

The Winterthur house was built between 1837 and 1839 by Jacques Antoine Bidermann and his wife, Evelina. Top: The house as it appeared in 1883, then inhabited by Col. Henry Algernon du Pont. Middle: The house in 1884, after the new roof was added (Louise and Henry Francis du Pont are playing on the lawn). Bottom: View of the house from the northeast showing the 1902 wing addition.

Louise du Pont

Henry Francis carried on an active correspondence throughout his life, a habit that may well have been spurred by his homesickness at Groton. One of his closest and most active correspondents was his sister, Louise. Three years older than Henry Francis, Louise was tutored at home by governesses while he attended boarding school. Her letters to him in this period begin affectionately, "Dearest Kid" or "Dear Hal." She wrote extensively about the family and social events and also began a dialogue on aesthetic matters that continued throughout their lives.

Henry Francis du Pont, only son of Henry Algernon, was born at Winterthur in 1880 and spent a happy childhood on the estate, roaming the property, observing nature, and collecting bird's eggs and mineral specimens. He and his sister, Louise, both fondly recalled the careful tutelage of their parents, who insisted that they learn the proper botanical names for the many varieties of plants that grew on the Winterthur grounds. When Henry Francis was sent to Groton, a preparatory boarding school, in 1893, he experienced the most acute homesickness, not only for his family but also for the familiar fields, trees, and gardens of his beloved home. In a series of letters to his family, he poured out his pain. In one, he wrote, "I am homesick only during the day. I am so homesick now that I don't know what to do. Do not show this to anyone . . . I have come from the football. We have won 60 to nothing. If someone doesn't come to see me soon I will die of grief. Please come to see me. I cry sometimes so that I cannot write. Goodbye dear Papa and Mama, Your little Harry. I have hugged all the pages."

His father mixed empathy with advice in his replies: "You must know how thoroughly I appreciate your feelings and how much I wish that it were in my power to make you feel immediately happy and comfortable at school. Remember that I have been also in a position like yours and your grandfather too, before me. He went to the military school at Mount Airy in 1822 [when] he was only ten years old! Keep up your courage, my dear Harry, and try absolutely to interest yourself in your sur-roundings—in your lessons and in the com-panionship of the other boys—and this will make your new life easier for you." He added, "Mama sends a thousand affectionate messages and bids me tell you that she despatched a basket of fruit to you by express this morning."

Perhaps it was this homesickness for his family and Winterthur, in particular the Winterthur gardens where he had spent so many happy hours with his mother, father, and sister, that influenced Henry Francis's decision to enroll at Harvard's Bussey Institution, where he followed a course of study in horticulture. He hoped to pursue graduate studies at the School of Practical Agriculture and Horticulture in Briarcliff Manor, New York, following graduation. In the summer of 1902, however, as he helped his father oversee the renovations to the house that resulted in the addition of a large wing across the north end of the building, his mother grew very ill and died in the early fall. Her husband and children were devastat-ed: Pauline du Pont, described by one friend as "the kindest person I ever met" had been directly responsible for imbuing in her chil-dren a deep and enduring love for Winter-thur by teaching them at home in their early years and engaging them in the daily activi-ties of the estate, including flower and veg-etable gardening. Henry Francis recalled in later years that his mother thought of Winterthur as "a place where people live who love the country."

Henry Francis du Pont
As a student at Harvard's Bussey Institution, du Pont indulged his love of nature by studying horticulture. For one of his courses, he wrote a paper entitled "Development of a Country Place, 1849–1902." Ironically, in light of his future achievements, he received a "B" grade.

*H*enry Francis, united in grief with his father, decided not to continue his formal horticulture studies after his graduation from Harvard in 1903 but to remain at Winterthur and assist in the management of the property. In the ensuing years, he not only relieved his father of many of the day-to-day chores but worked with him in the continual improvement of the garden. In 1906 Henry Algernon won election to the United States Senate and spent increasing amounts of time in Washington, D.C. As a result, he gradually turned the reins of Winterthur over to his son. They were reins Henry Francis never relinquished.

Between 1902 and 1914, many changes were made to both the farming operation and to the garden areas. A flurry of activity produced several new greenhouses, complete with ventilation, heating, and water systems, to join the original one built by the Bidermanns. In 1906 Henry Francis reported, "Although our range of glass is not large, it is subdivided into many small houses and we grow many varieties of plants," including chrysanthemums, figs, and ferns. Through the years, he worked hard to produce a range of glass that *was* large, adding four additional greenhouses plus cold frames (glass enclosures used to protect plants and seedlings) in 1924, two dahlia houses in 1930, and, during World War II, two greenhouses for growing peas, beans, and carrots. Even after

Greenhouses

Du Pont's expansion of Winterthur's gardening operations necessitated the addition of modern greenhouses for the propagation of vegetables, fruits, and other plants. The old garden area around the greenhouses was then developed into a series of terraced gardens where du Pont could experiment with bloom sequences and the massing of plants with closely related blossom colors.

Left: Henry Francis du Pont with one of his prize bulls.

Winterthur became a public museum in 1951, additional houses were added, including one for mushrooms, eventually totaling twenty-seven. All the greenhouses and related structures were arranged in two clusters located halfway up hills on either side of the Clenny Run stream. Thus, the formal appointment of Henry Francis as manager of the farms in 1914 was recognition not only of his considerable contribution of time and energy to the Winterthur estate but also of his talent for setting goals and working tirelessly to achieve them.

As Henry Francis began the work that was to engage most of his attention over the next ten years, he was influenced by philosophical models that reflected his goals for Winterthur. One was the agricultural tradition inherited from his du Pont ancestors, who saw the cultivation of land and the development of superior strains of plants and animals as the most desirable of all callings in life. The other was the model of the English country estates, many of which he would visit on extended trips to England. English country estates were more than just large expanses of land and palace-like houses. Rather, they were complete communities with many, if not most, essential foodstuffs cultivated on the grounds, including beef cattle, hogs, sheep, dairy cattle, poultry, vegetables, and fruits. Many of the estates also included large garden areas designed not only to ensure a constant supply of fresh flowers for the house but also to provide quiet retreats for the owner, his family, and guests. As Mark

Girouard, author of *Life in the English Country House: A Social and Architectural History* (1978), has explained, "The image of abundance is one of the most powerful of those connected with country houses; abundance flowing into the house, for the benefit of the families who lived in them and their guests, and out of them to the families living on the estate; abundance derived from woods, lakes, and rivers; and above all abundance of flowers, fruits, and vegetables in and from country-house orchards and gardens."

With these models in his mind, Henry Francis tackled the reorganization of the Winterthur estate. His father and grandfather had received rental income and food products from tenant farmers in return for certain services. Each farm, now part of a unified management system under Henry Francis's supervision, began to specialize in raising one or two kinds of farm product: one farm raised sheep, another hogs and beef cattle, a third farm horses, and another turkeys. Specific fields were reserved for growing crops to feed all the livestock: alfalfa, corn, barley, and hay as well as sugar beets, oats, and soybeans were all grown at one time or another.

The bulk of du Pont's time and attention, however, centered on improving the dairy operation begun by his father. He had devoted countless hours to developing, perfecting, and recording the progress of his wild garden of spring bulbs, and now he put the same forces to work to produce a better breed

Biltmore Estate

By emulating the English country estate, the du Ponts were following a tradition already well established among wealthy landowning families in America. George Washington Vanderbilt, grandson of the commodore, constructed a monumental country estate near Asheville, North Carolina, in the 1890s. In addition to maintaining a large piece of land and an imposing house, Vanderbilt created a dairy herd and working farm at Biltmore—necessary estate accessories according to the English formula. At a time when industrialization was overpowering urban areas in America, a farm or country place became a desirable retreat from the city. Dairying and farming were equated with an idyllic, healthful life, and families such as the Vanderbilts and the du Ponts were willing to take up the challenge of running those operations on a grand scale.

of Holstein, one that would produce milk with the highest butterfat content possible. His father heartily supported this goal, writing, "It won't cost as much as owning a yacht and it might do a lot for humanity."

Prizewinning Holsteins

In the 1910s, du Pont began purchasing the finest Holsteins from breeders across the country. He established a carefully controlled breeding program and registry tests for milk production. By 1926 the herd consisted of 300 registered Holsteins, and average milk production was 11,000 pounds per year per cow. A Winterthur cow, Winterthur Boast Ormsby Ganne, broke the fat yield record in 1933 by producing 1,004.2 pounds of butterfat from 23,444.6 pounds of milk. Her daily average, therefore, was 64 pounds of milk and 2.75 pounds of butterfat, or the equivalent today of 4.28% milk.

After studying the available research, Henry Francis began a systematic breeding program that involved the purchase of proven Holstein sires and the interbreeding of the best cows and bulls. This approach to breeding consistently produced results that broke records in the registry of the Holstein-Friesian Association of America.

A necessary part of this project involved the building of state-of-the-art barns on the Winterthur property. To direct this project, du Pont hired Elmer Humphries, a partner in an upstate New York firm that specialized in concrete construction and had experience building dairy barns. The new barns provided the herd with all the creature comforts, including reinforced concrete floors for insulation from dampness, fireproof doors at the hay chutes, and an elaborate ventilation and temperature-control system. They also featured Palladian windows, affording the workers an unparalleled view of the rolling meadows and forests of the Winterthur estate from the top of Farm Hill. When the barns were completed in 1917, du Pont named Humphries the superintendent of Winterthur Farms and added several staff, including a farm manager, resident veterinarian, dairy manager, and herdsman.

The Barns

To facilitate the expansion of his prizewinning herd of Holstein cattle, du Pont commissioned the construction of state-of-the-art barns. The modern facilities, which included the main barn, a creamery, a test barn, a calf barn, a heifer barn, a bull barn, and six barns for wintering young stock, could accommodate more than 400 head of cattle.

Across from the dairy barn, Humphries supervised the building of a creamery that could process 10,000 pounds of milk a day. An electric cable tramway capable of transferring six milk cans at a time connected the second level of the dairy barn to the top of the creamery, where the milk was sterilized and pasteurized before being sold to a local dairy and to employees on the estate. Sold as "Winterthur Special Holstein Milk" in bottles carrying the motto "Milk for Better Babies from Winterthur Farms," the milk was celebrated throughout the local area for its high quality.

To ensure the proper supervision of his prized herd, du Pont also had three workers' homes built near the dairy barn: one for the creamery man, another for the herdsman, and the third for the farm manager. The farm manager's home was also used as the farm office, which housed the diary records in a huge safe. The house is still in use today; it has been converted to offices for members of the Winterthur Garden Department.

Winterthur Dairy Operation

Winterthur's creamery housed a bottling room, an eight-ton ice plant, a cold storage room, and a laboratory for the chemical and bacteriological examination of all milk produced. An electric cable brought cans of milk from the barn to the processing area.

Housing for the farm staff was not the only amenity added to the estate at this time. In 1917 a clubhouse was constructed halfway up Farm Hill as a community gathering place for the growing number of employees who lived at Winterthur. Country estates were, by their very nature, removed from cities and towns, and many owners attempted to provide all the elements of a self-sufficient community on their properties. Winterthur, for example, offered its employees work, housing, some food, and a social center. The clubhouse contained a good-size auditorium, complete with stage, which at various times served as a meeting place for Sunday school and the Holstein-Friesian Association of America.

Life on the Winterthur estate was not all gardening and farming; it included entertaining on a grand scale as well. As a very eligible bachelor, Henry Francis was in demand socially, and he stood in place of his mother at the dinner parties given frequently at Winterthur. Du Pont demonstrated his skill as a host early on; one satisfied guest wrote in 1909, "You ought to have a prize for the wonderful gift you have, of getting together such charming and congenial people." One of these "congenial people," Eleanor Roosevelt, wrote in her 1915 "bread-and-butter" note, "The place and the garden are so lovely and I shall long remember the beauty of it all with pleasure." Many visitors during this period were English aristocrats whose estates the elder and younger du Pont had visited on trips to England. After spending a weekend at Winterthur in 1909, the son of Lord and Lady Elcho wrote, "This letter is to thank you for my visit to Winterthur which I really enjoyed very much indeed. The country and the church and the life generally reminded me very much of England."

Du Pont's bachelor days came to an end in 1916 when he married Ruth Wales of New York, a match greeted with much happiness by their many friends and family. Marriage meant the establishment of a New York apartment for the newlyweds and summer retreats to Southampton, Long Island, thus decreasing the time that du Pont spent at Winterthur. Nevertheless, he continued to oversee the dairy herd's breeding program and the refinement of the garden areas and always thought of Winterthur as his home.

In 1923, as part of his ongoing attempts to improve the herd, du Pont, accompanied by Ruth, traveled to Shelburne Farms in Vermont to visit the Watson Webb family and to take a close look at their dairy operation. The most memorable moment of the trip occurred not in the fields or barns, however, but in the home of Webb's daughter-in-law, Electra Havemeyer Webb, who collected American decorative arts. This was the moment, as du Pont loved to recount afterward, when he fell in love with American antiques and decided to collect them. "I hadn't thought of American furniture at all, I went upstairs [at Electra Webb's] and saw this dresser . . . this pine dresser and I thought it was charming, quite lovely. It just took my breath away. I had never seen pine furniture,

Ruth Wales du Pont
On June 24, 1916, Henry Francis du Pont married Ruth Wales of New York. Du Pont and his new bride both loved the countryside and enjoyed traveling, though Ruth devoted much of her time to raising their two daughters, Pauline Louise, born in 1918, and Ruth Ellen, born in 1922.

Web Dresser

While visiting the Vermont home of Mrs. J. Watson Webb in 1923, Henry Francis du Pont became "fascinated by the colors of a pine dresser filled with pink Staffordshire plates." This visit is said to have inspired du Pont to begin collecting American antiques. Following Webb's death in 1960, her children gave the inspirational dresser and Staffordshire service to du Pont. It is now on display at Winterthur.

or heard of it in fact."

On the same trip, the du Ponts also visited well-known decorator Henry Sleeper at his summer home, called Beauport, in Gloucester, Massachusetts. He had converted it into a showcase for American antiques and displayed objects in rooms made up of architectural fragments from American interiors, including paneling, doors, windows, and fireplaces. There du Pont's interest in Americana was further fueled by the artful displays Sleeper had created in his home: collections of American glass displayed in a window where the natural light set them aglow; a Chinese room, complete with hand-painted Chinese wallpaper and American Chippen-dale furniture in the Chinese taste; and "themed" rooms that grouped various related objects.

Inspired by Shelburne Farms and Beauport, du Pont began to devote considerable time to learning about and buying American furniture and other objects made or used in early America. He decided to build himself "an American house" and chose a site in Southampton, Long Island, where his family had summered for several years. He named it Chestertown House. Situated on the beach overlooking Long Island Sound,

Chestertown House was soon overflowing with examples of early American architecture and antiques.

In the midst of pursuing this new interest in American antiques, Henry Francis suffered a great loss, the death of his father, on the last day of the year in 1926. In his eighty-eight years of life, Henry Algernon du Pont had compiled a record of remarkable achievements. Highlights included graduating first in his class from West Point and being awarded the Congressional Medal of Honor for bravery at the Battle of Cedar Creek in the Civil War. When he returned to civilian life, he served as a vice-president of the DuPont Company and supported the sale of the company to three cousins who would restructure it into a modern industrial power. He served as president of the Wilmington and Northern Railroad and, always active in local politics, was elected a United States Senator from 1906 to 1917. He also imbued his children with his love of horticulture, farming, and antiques.

Like his son, however, Henry Algernon du Pont's many activities never interfered with his devotion to the Winterthur property, and to the end of his life, he maintained an active interest in both the garden and farm. This was recognized in his obituary in the Wilmington *Morning News*, which read, in part, "He had a deep interest in every phase of farming and a broad understanding and sympathy with agri-cultural problems."

Chestertown House
Built in Southampton, Long Island, Chestertown House was the summer home of Henry Francis du Pont and his family.

Henry Algernon du Pont
In his later years, Henry Algernon du Pont devoted more and more of his time to gathering his family's history, becoming a skilled amateur genealogist in the process. He published three books on this history and was working on a biography of Pierre Samuel du Pont when he died.

17

From Country Place to Grand Estate

After his father's death, du Pont began to identify himself when he traveled as "farmer" in guest books and on embarkation cards. He once laconically remarked, "If you're a farmer or whatnot, interested in a lot of things on the side which I am, you don't have much time." That he did not have "much time" comes as no surprise when considering the range of "things on the side" that were to continue to interest him until his death in 1969. In 1927, now the legal owner of his beloved home, he began an enormous expansion of the house, one that essentially tripled its size. A long, two-room-wide addition was attached to the south side of the house, rising eight stories at the far south end, in preparation for the display of the decorative arts of early America that he had avidly begun to collect. As he explained in later years, "I didn't believe the early-American arts and crafts had been given the recognition they deserved so I assembled examples of architecture, furniture, and widely divergent early-American materials of all sorts to show America as it had been."

Large projects were also being carried out simultaneously in the garden and on the estate. The addition of the large wing necessitated the redesign of many garden areas surrounding the original house, a project du Pont undertook with enthusiasm and foresight. He hired Marian Cruger Coffin, a good friend from his college days. Coffin had studied landscape architecture at the

A Grand Expansion

Following his father's death in 1926, du Pont began a massive expansion of the Winterthur house. Construction of the wing addition spanned three years and required careful planning. Creating a large structure that would fit comfortably into the hillside and join older portions of the house without overpowering them was a delicate architectural endeavor.

Left: Back pond at Winterthur.

**Marian Cruger
Coffin**

Lifelong friends, Coffin and
Henry Francis du Pont corre-
sponded frequently and collab-
orated on much of the landscape design work at Winterthur. Coffin's knowledge of
architectural landscape design
and du Pont's skill in selecting
plant varieties made them an
ideal working team, and the
success of their partnership
remains evident in the
Winterthur Garden.

Massachusetts Institute of Technology while
du Pont learned horticulture at Harvard's
Bussey Institution. Introduced in 1901 by
du Pont's sociable older sister, Louise, they
became fast friends and together visited gardens, arboreta, and flower shows in Boston
and abroad, particularly in England. Their
different focuses on these trips complemented
each other: Marian concentrated on landscape architecture, du Pont on the selection
and varieties of plants. This division of labor
became a hallmark of their later collabora-
tions at Winterthur: he deferred to her on
design issues, she to him on plant selection.
Marian Coffin was instrumental in the development of the Reflecting Pool area (then the
swimming pool), the Glade Garden, the
Peony Garden (originally the Iris Garden),
and, in the 1950s, the Sundial Garden.

The productive gardens at
Winterthur were also enlarged at this time.
Feeding Winterthur's large herd as well as the
other estate dwellers, both human and animal, required forty work horses and, later,
countless tractors. The large orchards grew
apples, peaches, cherries, and grapes. A five-
acre vegetable garden, as well as the greenhouses, contained every conceivable variety of
vegetable, including lima beans, corn, peas,
kale, potatoes, squash, and eggplant—the last
a particular favorite of Henry Francis. Mrs.
Olin Hance, who was in charge of the garden
after World War II, remembered that she
always tried to get the eggplant ready for
du Pont's July stay at Winterthur since he
loved it so much. Hance also recalled that she

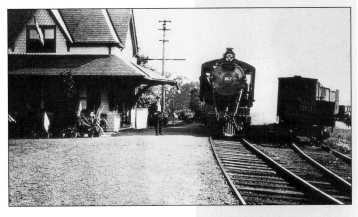

planted strawberries early so they could be picked in time for his birthday, May 27. According to her, Winterthur grew everything "except oysters." Hance also noted that du Pont always wanted to know the exact dates when anything bloomed, and it was part of her job to give him a list of blooming dates, which he then carefully recorded.

Food was frequently readied for shipping, as du Pont liked to enjoy Winterthur's bounty at each of his many homes—in Southampton, in New York City, and in Boca Grande, Florida. All received weekly shipments of milk and farm produce when he was in residence. Du Pont was provided with lists of vegetables, meat, poultry, and eggs before he left Winterthur, and he would mark on the list the quantities he wanted shipped to him. For one trip, he ordered an initial shipment of one hundred dozen eggs to be delivered to Boca Grande to be followed every other week by fifty dozen more. The Winterthur train station, built by Henry Algernon du Pont, facilitated this process: at one time, four trains a day brought supplies, workers, and visitors to Winterthur and took away the agricultural output of the estate.

In order to provide sufficient water for all of the garden and farm operations,

Train Station

Winterthur's train station was built in the mid 1890s by Henry Algernon du Pont, who had been appointed director of the Wilmington and Northern Railroad in 1878. Numerous freight trains and three passenger trains traveled across the Winterthur property each day.

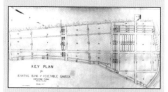

Vegetable Garden Plan, 1932

In the foreword to the *Winterthur Culinary Collection,* Pauline Harrison and Ruth Lord, the two daughters of Henry Francis and Ruth du Pont, recalled the bounty of the Winterthur estate. "When we were children, Winterthur was a working farm . . . Consequently, our family and others on the place ate the livestock raised there. We all ate heart, liver, sweetbreads, and tongue as a matter of course. Mother was especially fond of tripe and Father of pigs' feet. The vegetable gardens yielded every imaginable vegetable including one experimental variety each year . . . Our family liked beef and lamb very rare and wild duck cooked scarcely at all. Often these meats had to be returned to the oven for the benefit of those who did not share this taste."

du Pont dammed Clenny Run, a small stream that runs through the property on its way to the Brandywine River. This created several ponds, a landscape feature that not only served irrigation purposes but also enhanced an already pastoral landscape. An elaborate pipe system moved water from these ponds around the property for irrigation and firefighting needs. Howard Lattomus, a longtime employee, recalled the creation of the ponds, which necessitated the construction of a small house near the front pond for du Pont to sit in while observing and feeding the wild geese that took up residence at the inviting water holes.

The demands of overseeing an estate of more than 2,000 acres did not lessen the heavy schedule of entertaining begun during Henry Algernon's lifetime. Both Henry Francis and Ruth du Pont loved to give parties, many of which lasted for an entire weekend. The house and grounds, particularly the garden, provided the perfect settings for such gatherings. A frequent weekend guest to Winterthur once described the weekend parties: "You'd arrive, probably teatime, and there would be Ruth, behind the tea table, and you'd be having tea, and you'd probably play bridge before dinner, and certainly play bridge after dinner." She went on to note that she frequently lost her way in the house trying to find her room in the evening.

A visitor to Winterthur could look forward to inside sports such as bowling, squash, billiards, and bridge. Outside, tennis and croquet were played on courts near the

Pinetum, and a swimming pool was located at the bottom of the formal garden on the east side of the house, complete with changing rooms and speakers to allow music to be piped in for parties. Most important to Henry Francis was golf, which could be played on Winterthur's own golf course.

The golf course had been built in the late 1920s, shortly after du Pont inherited Winterthur from his father. In 1928 Henry Francis had contacted Devereaux Emmet, a New York golf course architect and contractor, writing, "I am thinking of building a nine-hole golf course on my place and would you come down within the next week or two and look over the place I have selected to see if you think anything worthwhile could be done there." Emmet hired Percy Vickers, originally from Scotland, to help build the course, and Vickers became Winterthur's first golf pro; he would stay on at Winterthur for forty years. In 1929 the golf course officially opened at a family party. Spread over eighty acres, the course consisted of 10 greens and 6,480 yards of fairway. It took a staff of seven men to care for the course in the summer; teenage boys living on the estate were recruited as caddies.

Golf Outing

A round of golf was a favorite weekend activity for guests at Winterthur. Du Pont himself was a devoted golfer and once exclaimed to Percy Vickers, Winterthur's golf pro, "Do you know anyone that loves this game better than I and plays it so damn badly!" In 1963 du Pont leased the course to a group of local businessmen who established the Bidermann Golf Course, now a private club.

Golf, then, was one of the favorite activities during a long weekend at Winterthur. On Sundays guests often played golf accompanied by opera music, which was broadcast loudly from speakers located in the nearby woods. Du Pont himself loved the game, and he played often. A fair player, he achieved every golfer's dream on a memorable day in 1941 when he scored a hole-in-one.

In the evenings, guests were treated to formal dinners in the family dining room, a large room furnished in the federal style, complete with late eighteenth-century sideboards, a dining table, chairs, silver, and portraits. As the du Pont daughters described the scene: "At any time of year, our dining room table looked beautiful, with different sets of china, place mats, and flower arrangements . . . After dark, the room was lighted by candles, with candlesticks on the table and candelabra standing on the floor."

The du Ponts followed the French tradition of having many courses at each meal, so before each dinner party Henry Francis and Ruth du Pont consulted at length with the cook about what would be served. Henry Francis personally supervised the selection of china, placemats, and flower arrangements. Each week he determined which flowers would be at their peak during the coming weekend; he then made decisions about which linens and dishes would be used. Ruth drew on her skills as a warm and talented hostess in devising the seating plans; according to her daughters, she seemed to sense which individuals would enjoy talking with one another. If eight or more people were to be present at dinner, white porcelain place cards were used. Du Pont himself had a white porcelain menu holder at his place.

Another favorite activity for guests was visiting the magnificent gardens at Longwood in Pennsylvania, created by Pierre Samuel du Pont II, Henry Francis's second cousin. He, too, followed his ancestors' dictum of "tilling the soil" in a grand fashion. Pierre Samuel purchased a farm in the early 1900s, complete with park and arboretum, which he developed over the years into a world-famous garden, one that remains to this day a favorite site for tourists and horticulturists.

Throughout the years Winterthur witnessed many special family occasions, including the debuts of both daughters as well as their weddings. One highlight was the du Ponts' twenty-fifth wedding anniversary celebration in 1941. It was an evening long to be remembered. As one guest recounted: "Seventy dined at a table built around the swimming pool. A silver cloth was used with an edging of pink rambler roses on the pool side and silvered chairs . . . The pool was lighted from the bottom and in the pool was a silver boat with a silver sail, the edges of the

Silver Anniversary Celebration
Sixty-eight guests gathered at Winterthur in 1941 to celebrate Henry Francis and Ruth du Pont's twenty-fifth wedding anniversary. Above: A young boy practices maneuvering the boat that carried the evening's musical entertainment—an accordion player who serenaded guests as they dined poolside.

Azalea Woods
Du Pont selected Kurume
azaleas in predominantly pastel
shades and grouped them
throughout Azalea Woods in
subtly contrasting color relationships. Under du Pont's careful
orchestration, the area eventually grew to encompass eight
acres.

boat being outlined with the same pink rambler roses, and a boy dressed in a silver sailor suit with blue collar, paddled with silver oars. Felix Restive, an accordion player, was in the stern of the boat and the boy rowed him from one side of the table to the other while he sang and played."

While many of the weekend guests to Winterthur were members of the du Ponts' social set, Henry Francis also established close friendships with the many antiques dealers, architects, gardeners, and farmers he interacted with in the course of business. In 1936 he invited Joe Kindig, an antiques dealer from York, Pennsylvania, for the weekend, telling him, "You won't need to bring any evening clothes, as we will be going to the wrestling matches." Du Pont was also the master of the thoughtful gesture, something he learned from his mother. Years after he discovered the Kurume azaleas that he used so successfully in Winterthur's Azalea Woods, he wrote to Robert T. Brown, owner of Cottage Gardens Nursery on Long Island: "I shall always be grateful to you for those Kurume Azaleas you sold me years ago and I should like you to come down and see them and their children and grandchildren. I imagine they will be in bloom between May 11th and 16th." Despite his failing health, Brown happily journeyed to Winterthur to view his azalea's progeny. Afterward he expressed his deep appreciation for du Pont's thoughtfulness: "I want to tell you how much I enjoyed my visit with you going over the Azaleas. The display was such a marvelous one that I will never forget it and I wish now to thank you for very much for the opportunity of seeing them."

Du Pont also used these visits as a way of increasing his knowledge about antiques, farming, and gardening. In 1951 he invited Henry Skinner, then a doctoral student in horticulture at the University of Pennsylvania and later director of the National Arboretum in Washington, D.C., for a weekend: "I am very keen to hear about all your travels and ask innumerable questions."

One of the most famous visitors to Winterthur came in 1961, ten years after Winterthur became a public institution. Mrs. John F. Kennedy asked Henry Francis du Pont to serve as chairman of her newly formed Fine Arts Committee for the White House, and du Pont subsequently invited her to visit him at Winterthur. Albert Feliciani, who grew up at Winterthur, remembers being asked to cut a bouquet of lilies-of-the-valley to present to Jacqueline Kennedy when she arrived. Following the visit, Mrs. Kennedy wrote to Henry Francis to express her admiration for his achievement: "I just

Visit from the First Lady

On May 8, 1961, the first lady, Jacqueline Kennedy (shown here with du Pont and Dana Taylor), visited Winterthur to study its collections and rooms in connection with the refurnishing of the White House. Du Pont served as chairman of the Fine Arts Committee for the White House.

can't believe that it was possible for anyone to ever do such a thing." She added, poignantly, in view of subsequent events, "I now have an ambition for our old age—for us to be gate-keepers at Winterthur."

All of this activity—in the house, in the garden, and on the farm—required increasing numbers of workers to manage the multitude of ongoing projects. Dairy work-ers, farmers, gardeners, carpenters, cooks, maids, a butler, and even two footmen all contributed to the efficient operations of the

Winterthur Workers

As a young man, du Pont befriended the farmworkers, gardeners, and greenhousemen and helped them with their work on the estate. In this way he acquired his first practical experience in gardening and animal husbandry.

estate. At one time during the period between the two world wars, more than 250 people lived on the estate in more than ninety hous-es. Most of the houses were newly built or were existing farm structures refur-bished by Henry Algernon in the late nine-teenth and early twentieth centuries. One, a late eighteenth-century, federal-style brick farmhouse was built by Joseph Chandler and his son Benjamin. It was acquired by Henry Algernon du Pont in 1916, along with 100 acres of land, from the Chandler family. In 1958 Henry Francis remodeled the house to provide a spacious home for the director of

Winterthur Museum. Today, in the kitchen, evidence remains of the house's earliest occupancy on one of the windowpanes; the name "Benjamin" is roughly scratched into the glass.

For Winterthur employees, life on the Winterthur estate involved much more than work. The children of employees, many of whom would go on to work at Winterthur themselves, had complete access to the estate grounds and enjoyed sledding and ice skating on the ponds in the winter, fishing in the summer, and bike riding or hiking all year round. In addition, there were opportunities for gainful employment for the children. As a small boy, Albert Feliciani lived with his family at Montchanin, a small village on the Winterthur estate named for Henry Francis du Pont's great-great-great-grandmother. Their home was one of the first worker's houses at Winterthur to be modernized. He was assigned small jobs on the property, such as picking pansies from the cutting garden, weeding the golf greens, and caddying for du Pont and his guests.

A year at Winterthur was filled with special events, parties, sports, and games. There was a Winterthur baseball team, complete with uniforms. A former carpenter, an especially good pitcher, remembers being hired just in time for the baseball season.

Chandler Farm
The Winterthur property is made up of many farms acquired over the years by the du Ponts. Existing buildings were adapted to serve the needs of the expanding estate, often becoming housing for workers. The Chandler family farm was purchased in 1916, and the original federal-style brick farmhouse (top) today serves as the director's residence (bottom).

Play Ball

Distanced from the amenities available in cities and towns, Winterthur became a largely self-sufficient community, with its own laundry and carpenter, blacksmith, and butcher shops. Employees formed a baseball team (complete with uniforms) and a band, gathered for dances and holiday parties, and took advantage of the estate's social facilities, which included a clubhouse and a large auditorium for concerts and Sunday school classes.

More informally, employees gathered to play boccie ball and soccer. There were also Saturday night parties, movies, dances, bridge and bingo games, and musical events. The highlight of the year, however, was always the Winterthur Christmas party. The Christmas parties, begun by Henry Algernon du Pont in the main house, grew so large that in 1917 they were moved to the newly finished clubhouse. Known informally as "Mr. Harry's party," the event included special entertainment personally selected by du Pont. Over the years, Bozo the Clown, Chief Halftone, the Poodle Symphony, and numerous magicians added to the general gaiety. The main event of the party was, of course, the gift-giving. The du Ponts made a point of being present to hand out gifts to employees in appre-

ciation of their loyal service. Du Pont himself made special arrangements with a local department store, Wanamaker's, to allow him to shop after-hours for the multitude of presents necessary for sometimes as many as 210 children. Toys, sleds, baseballs and bats, books, and games headed the list. The adults received turkeys (raised on the estate), apples, and candy.

Christmas Dinner

Daughters Pauline Harrison and Ruth Lord fondly recall the family Christmas dinner tradition: "On Christmas night, there was a suckling pig crisply roasted with an apple in its mouth, which followed stew of diamondback terrapin, a kind of turtle which crawled around in our cellar before being dispatched ... Among the wineglasses, a glass of sherry was provided at each place to be added to the turtle stew as desired. Another Christmas dish was a large roast turkey with chestnut stuffing surrounded by homemade sausage. This tasted even better than the Thanksgiving turkey, probably because of Christmas stockings and the piney smell of the Christmas tree."

A Country Place Museum

From the moment that Henry Francis du Pont graduated from Harvard and returned to Winterthur in 1903, he never ceased to experiment, improve, refine, and change. Whether on the farm, with the dairy herd, in the garden, or with his decorative arts collection, he always looked ahead with an eye toward making things better. Thus, it is not surprising that he began to think about Winterthur's future almost from the moment he inherited the estate. As early as 1930, he established the Winterthur Corporation with the intent of maintaining Winterthur in perpetuity as "a museum and arboretum for the education and enjoyment of the public." What du Pont meant by this is not precisely clear. Certainly, the concept of making Winterthur a public institution evolved over time. In 1932, when he wrote to Thomas Waterman, a young architect, to proclaim that "my house is completely finished," he still saw Winterthur primarily as his home rather than as a potential museum. By 1938, however, after having involved Waterman in the complete refurbishment of his father's Victorian interiors, his ideas had clearly changed. He wrote to William Sumner Appleton of the Society for the Preservation of New England Antiquities, saying, "This [Winterthur] may be a museum some day."

About the same time, Beverley Robinson, du Pont's attorney and cousin, advised that the position of Winterthur as a "charitable corporation" would be strength-

Left: Winterthur Museum.

Charles F. Montgomery

Charles F. Montgomery, a dealer and pewter specialist from Wallingford, Connecticut, came to Winterthur in 1949 to help catalogue Henry Francis du Pont's impressive furniture collection. In 1954 he was appointed the first director of Winterthur Museum following du Pont's recommendation, which characterized Montgomery as "hard-headed, capable, and an indefatigable worker" with an "intense enthusiasm for antiques and what they mean and have meant in the American way of life."

ened if the house were opened for some kind of exhibition. Thus, in 1941 it was decided to open parts of the house for public view on the first Tuesday, Wednesday, and Thursday afternoons of each month. In 1942 advertisements were placed in publications such as *Museum News,* and visitors began making reservations to see du Pont's collection.

It seems clear that at this time du Pont still envisioned Winterthur becoming a museum only after his death. At some point, however, he changed his mind and began to plan in earnest for transforming Winterthur into a public institution in his own lifetime. He described the process by which this change occurred in a magazine interview in 1951, the year Winterthur opened to the public: "I always knew what I wanted Winterthur to be, but I never thought it could happen until I popped off. Then one day I got to thinking, if I want a museum here I ought to see the job through myself. Besides, I suspected there would be some fun connected with it, and I wanted to be in on it." He offered a slightly different explanation in an interview with Harlan Phillips of the Archives of American Art in 1961, explaining, "I want to have a thing going, have it established and see it going. Then I'll know what I wanted to do was done." In a 1962 letter to Phillips, he confessed, "I realized that the collection was too good to be dispersed after my death and hence the idea of a museum gradually came to me."

In order to effect the transformation

34

of Winterthur from a private estate to a public museum, du Pont worked on two fronts. First, he formalized his professional relationships with Charles F. Montgomery, a dealer and collector, and Joseph Downs, the curator of American art at the Metropolitan Museum of Art and hired them to work as Winterthur employees, assigning them the task of cataloguing his antiques collection. Second, he commissioned his good friend and architectural collaborator, Thomas Waterman, to build a "cottage" for him and Ruth to move into when Winterthur opened to the public. All were fortuitous choices. In Montgomery and Downs, he brought to Winterthur two of the foremost talents of their day in the emerging field of American decorative arts. Eventually, Downs became the first curator of the museum, Montgomery the first director. One of Montgomery's first acts was to establish the Winterthur Program in Early American Culture, a graduate program run in conjunction with the University of Delaware that established Winterthur as the premier research institution for the study of America's material heritage.

The spot chosen by Waterman and du Pont for the latter's new residence was the site of the original farmhouse on the Winterthur property. The new multilevel house was built in the English Regency style and overlooked Clenny Run to the south and the garden to the north. From his bedroom windows, du Pont could look up the hill to the barns on Farm Hill, down the slope to naturalized plantings of daffodils along

Joseph Downs

Initially hired by du Pont to prepare a comprehensive catalogue of the furniture collection, Joseph Downs became Winterthur's first curator in January 1949. He was the logical choice for this important position. He came to Winterthur with more than two decades of museum experience, including serving as curator of the American Wing at the Metropolitan Museum of Art.

Henry F. du Pont House

Du Pont moved his family into what is today referred to as the H. F. House at the end of 1950 in preparation for the opening of Winterthur Museum in 1951. He furnished the house with English and French furniture from his New York apartment.

Clenny Run, and over to the original house, now the Henry Francis du Pont Winterthur Museum. Thus, all three of his consuming interests were clearly in view.

Once the house had opened as a museum with suitably impressive flair on October 30, 1951, du Pont lessened his involvement in the museum itself. Although the staff was careful to consult him on all matters, he trusted their judgment and interfered as little as possible. He remained, however, to the end of his days, the "head gardener" and continued to list his occupation as "farmer" on all official documents.

Once established in his new home on Clenny Run, du Pont continued to plan for the future of the Winterthur property. In the 1950s, he sold a large parcel of land, consisting mainly of the old Martin farm, to the Wilmington Country Club and another tract located across the Kennett Pike to the Methodist Country Home, a retirement community. He leased 141 acres to a group of Wilmington businessmen in 1963 for the creation of the Bidermann Golf Course. In 1965 a large parcel of land between Winterthur and the Brandywine River was conveyed to the state of Delaware and made into Brandywine Creek State Park, a nature center with walking trails. This land had originally been put "in trust" by Henry Algernon du Pont for younger members of the family. Altogether, this combination of sale and bequest created a wide protective band of open land between Winterthur and the encroaching development of Wilmington. It also reduced the Winterthur estate to a more manageable 983 acres. Of these, 192 remained cropland, 259 continued to be used as grazing pastures, 163 stayed woodlands, and 61 were cultivated gardens.

Du Pont also made provisions for the future of the Winterthur farm. He added a codicil to his will in 1959 arranging for the Winterthur Corporation to receive his "herd of Holstein cattle and all other livestock, poultry, horses, carriages, carts, harness and stable equipment, and all dairy, farm, agricultural and other implements." The document went on to state, "In the interest of preserving and realizing the maximum value of such herd of Holstein cattle, I recommend that Winterthur Corporation arrange for the sale of such herd promptly after my death or promptly after receiving the possession thereof from my Executors in the distribution of

Head Gardener

A passionate recordkeeper, du Pont diligently kept track of the blooming sequences of his plantings so that he could improve their positioning and extend their visual impact. Winterthur's self-appointed "head gardener," he regularly strolled through the grounds in the early morning, charting routes that would highlight the most spectacular garden views for visitors.

my estate." It could not have been easy for du Pont to reach this conclusion. As late as 1962, he explained, "Somehow or other, as I think I've said before, I've always been interested in this sort of thing [breeding cattle], and I think I'll keep on with it." In deciding to part with the herd and terminate the farm operation, du Pont acknowledged the great cost and time commitment necessary for their maintenance and the resources (human and financial) they were taking away from the museum.

Ruth Wales du Pont died in 1967, leaving Henry Francis alone in the cottage. His children were living in New York, as were his grandchildren, and the future of his life's work was secure. Surely he could rest now. Yet, old habits die hard, and du Pont remained active until the time of his death. He continued to "keep on with" his interest in cattle, and in November 1968, the Holstein-Friesian Association of America notified him that he had once again earned the Progressive Breeders Registry Award. Although the museum's professional staff ran the museum on a day-to-day basis, the major decisions remained his. In early 1969, he approved the purchase of architecture from a home in Milledgeville, Georgia, to be

installed in the museum in a space formerly occupied by the estate's kitchen, and whenever he was in residence at Winterthur, he walked in the garden, making countless notes for himself and his gardeners on bloom dates and plantings.

In the spring of 1969, when he was eighty-nine years old, du Pont visited Europe in the company of several friends and members of his family. According to one of the trip's participants, it was a "wonderful trip . . . a happy trip." When they returned, du Pont went immediately to his home in Florida, where he became ill. Sensing that at his age this might be his final illness, du Pont's family and friends made arrangements for his prompt return to Winterthur. When he reached there, he was met in the hallway by his longtime butler, Maurice. According to a friend, he asked Maurice,

Disbanding the Herd

As the demands of the museum increased in the 1950s and 1960s, du Pont gradually reduced the size of the Winterthur herd and instructed the Winterthur Corporation to dismantle the breeding operation upon his death. In 1969, in compliance with the terms of du Pont's will, Winterthur's famed herd of Holstein cattle was sold at auction.

"Am I at Winterthur?" When Maurice assured him that he was, indeed, at Winterthur, du Pont visibly relaxed. He died the next day, April 11, 1969.

Henry Francis du Pont's legacy continues to this day. In the museum, a new generation of curators, conservators, and educators collect, conserve, and interpret American decorative arts for the enjoyment of the public, almost 200,000 of whom arrive every year to take a tour, attend a special event, or stroll in the garden. In the years since his death, the collection has grown to more than 89,000 objects, with new acquisitions made according to the same principles that guided du Pont: rarity, beauty, historical association, and history of ownership. After experiencing a period of benign neglect, the magnificent naturally landscaped garden has been revived and restored in accord not only with du Pont's original design intent but also with his horticultural philosophy, which included continual experimentation to find the best possible varieties and combinations of plants.

Although the farm is no longer a focal point of the estate, it remains an integral part of the visitor's experience at Winterthur. Whether riding through the garden on a tram, walking the shady paths of Azalea Woods, or standing in a period room gazing out a window, visitors are reminded of Winterthur's past: the barns can be seen on the crest of Farm Hill, sharply silhouetted against a winter sky; many of the former workers' houses still dot the landscape; and the rolling fields along the back drive recall a

time when acres of grain helped feed a large livestock operation.

Above: Front pond at Winterthur.

Henry Francis du Pont never enjoyed speaking in public, and he confined his writing to personal correspondence whenever possible. He preferred to let his achievements speak for him. Thus, it is not surprising that he was able to sum up his feelings for his life-long home in very few words. Towards the end of his life, he told an interviewer, "I was born at Winterthur and have always loved everything connected with it."

Mary Pauline Foster du Pont
with her children, Louise Evelina
and Henry Francis, about 1890.